YOUR KNOWLEDGE HAS

Bibliographic information published by the German National Library:

The German National Library lists this publication in the National Bibliography; detailed bibliographic data are available on the Internet at http://dnb.dnb.de .

Imprint:

Copyright © 2011 GRIN Verlag, Open Publishing GmbH
Print and binding: Books on Demand GmbH, Norderstedt Germany
ISBN: 9783668267947

This book at GRIN:

http://www.grin.com/en/e-book/194101/online-requirements-engineering-at-runti-me-an-overview-of-the-different

Bekim Meta

Online Requirements Engineering at runtime. An overview of the different supporting frameworks

GRIN Publishing

GRIN - Your knowledge has value

Since its foundation in 1998, GRIN has specialized in publishing academic texts by students, college teachers and other academics as e-book and printed book. The website www.grin.com is an ideal platform for presenting term papers, final papers, scientific essays, dissertations and specialist books.

Visit us on the internet:

http://www.grin.com/

http://www.facebook.com/grincom

http://www.twitter.com/grin_com

Table of Contents

Requirements Engineering at runtime - Online RE

Bekim Meta

University of Zurich
Seminar in Requirements Engineering

Abstract. The paper gives a brief introduction into different frameworks and concepts to support requirements engineering at runtime, also known as - Online Requirements Engineering. Describing these frameworks will give us an overview of current research trends in this challenging topic of requirements engineering. As the current research shows, designing such kind of frameworks significantly challenges the role of requirements engineering.

Keywords: Online Requirements Engineering, OnlineRE, dynamically adaptive systems. OnlineRE frameworks

1 Introduction

Requirements engineering at runtime is one of the challenging areas of requirements engineers. To specify requirements, apart from current system behavior the engineers have to additionally describe possible changes that the system and its environment may encounter in the future. The more possible adaptation possibilities are described, the better is the expected behavior of the system. Ensuring that the requirements specification is complete, becomes increasingly difficult and complicated. The requirements continuously change and the environments are getting more and more complex. To deal with such complexity, stable and continuously adaptable systems are needed. The user of the system should receive optimal results at any time. This paper should give an overview of existing work and highlight open points for future research.

1

2 Terms and Definitions

2.1 Important terms and definition used in the paper

The purpose of this chapter is to give a definition of some key terms that are used in different aspects in this paper. Most of them play a prominent role in runtime requirements engineering.

Requirements Monitoring: Determines the degree to which a system satisfies its requirements [1]. It also detects conditions that might conduct to a requirement violation.

Adaptive Monitoring: A monitoring technique to reduce monitoring overhead while achieving acceptable levels of monitoring accuracy [2]. The monitoring configuration is updated continuously depending on the monitored system at runtime.

Adaptive Sampling: A technique to minimize the monitoring costs by continuously adapting the frequency of the sensors gather monitoring data [2]. While system and environmental conditions stay constant, the monitoring frequency is very low. If the environmental conditions change, the monitoring frequency increases accordingly.

DAS (Dynamic Adaptive System): It is a computer based system (CBS) that: is capable of recognizing that the domain with which it shares an interface has changed and is capable of changing its behavior to adapt to the changing conditions. [3]

Goal oriented requirements engineering: The goal oriented requirements engineering is a new approach in requirements engineering. It makes explicit the - why - of requirements [4]. Before this approach the requirements on data and operation were just there. Why they were there and whether they were sufficient was not captured [5]. A seminal work by Lamsweerde [6] gives a deep explanation on this goal-oriented requirements engineering approach.

Goals vs. Requirements: A goal is defined as a fixed objective of a service, whereas a requirement is a more volitive concept that can be influenced by the context [6]. A requirement represents one of the possible ways of achieving a goal. It represents a more concrete short-term objective that is directly achievable through actions performed by one or more agents. E.g. If we take an online shop, one goal could be to maximize usability of the system , which is very abstract. By contrast a requirement could be – the display must show both, the current shopping basket and a list of available options.

Genetic Algorithm: A genetic algorithm is a stochastic, research based technique for generating solutions in optimization problems in large solution spaces [2].

Context aware services: The context awareness means the ability of a particular service to adapt itself to a continuously changing environment.

Development time vs. runtime: A software system is permanently changed and adapted, improved throughout its lifetime. Thus its difficult to make a clear distinction between development time and runtime. In contrast a software release is a finalized version of a software system at a given point in time. A new system is developed based on new requirements and previous release (bug fixes included). Therefore the runtime of the software is starting when the development time is finished. The deployed release is used inside a customer organization.

Changing context: While analyzing requirements we cannot rely on assumptions about the world. It complicates the development of the software. An example adapted from Finkelsteins and Savignis work [5] gives a good explanation of a changing context, in the case of a context-aware mobile service. The changing context may entail:

Changing location: Not only the absolute location of one device can change, but also the relative location of two devices must be taken into consideration.

Changing bandwidth: bandwidth changes for mobile devices are often unpredictable.

Changing display characteristics: There are different mobile phones and devices in the market which have different display characteristics. E.g. PDAs, text-only mobile phones, smart-phones, etc.

Changing usage paradigm: For example from a user perspective having a full screen, button centered PDA, is very different from using a scroll-centered mobile phone.

Unknown target platform: Platforms may be unknown in advance and the services should anyway be able to dynamically adapt to the new context.

2.2 Definition of OnlineRE

Before going deeper into OnlineRE I will try to formulate a definition. The term 'OnlineRE' is a new term in the world of requirements engineering and there is no definition yet existing. After some research on requirements engineering at runtime, I define OnlineRE as follow:

OnlineRE is the task of monitoring, capturing, organizing, structuring and analyzing user requirements after the application has being deployed or installed at customer side.

As we can extract out of the definition above, OnlineRE starts from the moment on the customer has installed our software. All tasks from that moment on are considered to be part of requirements engineering at runtime.

3   RE at development time vs. RE at runtime

In this chapter I want to make a distingshment of requirements engineering at development time and requirements engineering at runtime. I will briefly give an overview of the requirements engineering at development time, and switch to what's relevant while doing requirements engineering at runtime.

3.1 RE at development time

At development time the requirements engineering process consists of different steps:

Requirements Elicitation: During the elicitation process we try to communicate with our customers, users and all other stakeholders to gather different software requirements. We try to do it as good as possible from different point of views. Possible techniques that are used here are interviews, questionnars, surveys etc. We can also visit the customer at his workplace and try to understand the requirements he might have. We try to find out constraints and how the current system (if there is one) might affect our software.

Requirements Modeling: After the elicitation the requirements modeling takes place. During this process we try to generate different system models to illustrate different point of views. One important part in this process is to find out how the system behaves, how it reacts to different events from outside. Helpful tasks in this process are also structuring the system in different parts and also modeling the system environment. Including traceability links [7] makes it much easier for the development and the customer to understand the dependencies to the requirements.

Requirements Specification: In the specification process we try to exactly describe and formulate the previously defined models. We can generate different prototypes which will help us in the next iteration to make the requirements more precise and eliminate or find new requirements from the stakeholders.

Requirements Validation: During the validation process we validate all gathered requirements. We try to find errors and correct them or validate them having the costs and development effort in mind. We also make sure if specific requirements can be done with current technology or not.

Requirements Management: In this process we document all the requirements and maintain them if there are changes or requirement updates during runtime. Most of the processes are done in several iterations until we get to a point where we say that all requirements are correct and accepted by the customer.

3.2 RE at runtime

Now we switch to RE at runtime. Currently most of researches in this topic of requirements engineering are focusing on how to monitor a software system and dynamically update it at runtime. That is why monitoring takes a key position in the frameworks I,Äôm going to talk about later in this paper. As I,Äôve had good personal experience using some other techniques and methods in a context of runtime requirements engineering, I decided to include them in my paper as well. The techniques I am going to introduce and explain in detail are the following:

Log File Analysis: Logs are the language the application uses to talk to us. That,Äôs why they are so attractive to be used at runtime to refine requirements, identify requirements violations and maybe gather new requirements. We can

4

analyze them in detail, extract requirements engineering relevant information out of them and use this information to increase usability and requirements satisfaction at runtime.

Integrated tools for user feedback: The next technique I‚Äôm introducing is integrated tools for user feedback, which shall make it easy to the software users to send us feedback regarding the usage of the application, requirements violations, improvements etc.

Log file analysis of interoperability modules:

This is quite similar with the – Log file Analysis – method. The difference here is that we use logs of other modules and applications or components our software interacts with. We can analyze them and try to find requirements violations. Now we will go deeper into the monitoring technique. As I mentioned above monitoring is a very important term in the OnlineRE context. In the following I will describe what monitoring is and what we can monitor at runtime. Monitoring in software systems is mostly used to monitor performance aspects of the software. Using monitoring in the context of requirements engineering is a new technique and is integrated in different frameworks regarding OnlineRE.

In the following few lines I will briefly show what can be monitored at runtime in an OnlineRE context.

Application Environment and Context: We can monitor the environment the application is installed or deployed on. We can monitor different parameters like bandwidth, operating system, browser name, browser version, memory available, cpu usage etc. All this data can be used to automatically update the application according to the context it is running on.

User Activity: For example on a web application we can monitor the browsing activity, clicking on different actions, the frequency of the usage of different features of the application. Having this kind of information we can restructure the application according to user activity.

Interoperability Modules: At runtime our software might interact with other modules, components of different applications. Monitoring this interaction can increase the stability of the software. The requirements of other interacting components might change during time, monitoring them will help us to dynamically refine existing requirements and if possible gather new requirements at runtime.

System Performance: Monitoring system performance was the start of monitoring techniques. Having performance data at runtime can help us to identify bottlenecks, memory usage of different parts of the software, cpu usage etc.

Error Logs: Most of applications produce errors which are written on error log files. Monitoring the errors can help us to identify requirement engineering specific errors and refine or update the requirements accordingly.

4 OnlineRE frameworks and techniques

In this chapter I will introduce and briefly explain some techniques which can be used in a runtime requirements engineering context, including their strengths and limitations. I will start with some of the frameworks used in different research projects and go on with some techniques coming from my side, also very useful in an onlineRE context.

4.1 Plato-RE

Plato - RE presented by Ramirez et al. [2, 12] detects conditions that might conduct to a requirement violation and dynamically generates new monitoring configurations at runtime. It is a computation-based approach to adaptively monitor software requirements. The framework continuously observes the running system components and sensors to make sure that all requirements are satisfied. It is able to detect conditions that might conduct to a requirements violation. This approach is very computationally expensive and requires a set of configuration parameters and preferences to be predefined at development time. Each configuration specifies another data gathering frequency from the components and active system sensors.

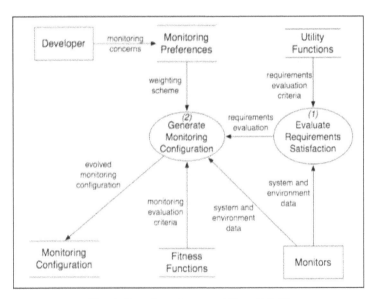

Fig. 1. Data flow diagram of Plato-RE [2]

Fig. 1 shows an overview of the data flow of Plato-RE [2]. As we can see it uses different data types to generate a new monitoring configuration. The figure illustrates how the data is generated from starting at design time until the requirements are monitored at runtime. At design time the developers specify preferences for monitoring the satisfaction of requirements, such as tradeoffs between costs and data accuracy. At runtime the system evaluates the degree of requirements satisfaction by applying utility functions. It also detects conditions conductive to a requirement violation. The utility functions continually produce new values. If these values drop below a user specified threshold, a trigger is invoked and Plato-RE generates a new monitoring configuration. As input data it accepts monitoring data, the values produced by utility functions and monitoring preferences. [2, 12] A dynamically adaptive systems (DAS) can use this configuration and tune the frequency parameter for the system components and sensors. Ramirez et al. [2] show a detailed explanation of this approach in their work. They demonstrate how developers may leverage it in a context of a running example.

Strengths

1. *Optimizes system behavior at runtime.*
   As the system permanently generates the best configuration it extremely saves system resources. E.g. a robot with several sensors can save power as Plato RE makes it possible to use adaptive monitoring and adaptive sampling (see terms and definitions).
2. *Dynamically updates the monitoring configuration.*
   The system does not have to be offline to generate a new monitoring configuration. It will dynamically generate it while the system is running.
3. *System variables are dynamically adjusted.*
   All system variables are adjusted to permanently have the best values according to the environment.
4. *Reduces monitoring costs.*
5. *Increases performance and application quality.*

Limitations

1. *Only applicable to non-functional requirements.*
   Plato RE can only adapt the system to increase performance or quality. The framework is not able to adapt the system to change the functionality according to the environment or the context.
2. *Small range of application domains.*
   The framework can not be used for any software domain. It is only used in domains where sensors are used to monitor the system environment, e.g. in robots.
3. *Computational intensive.*
   It uses a lot of utility and fitness functions to generate new monitoring configurations, therefore it is very computational expensive and requires a lot of system resources.
4. *Uses stochastic data, probability, predictions .*
   The framework uses genetic algorithms (see terms and definitions) to generate new configurations. Predictions may not always generate the right results.

4.2 Traceability Links

Traceability Links are used as a technique to manage the links from the requirements to the code and from the code to the requirements. Gotel and Finkelstein

[9] define traceability links as follow:

Requirements Traceability refers to the ability to describe and follow the life of a requirement, in both a forwards and backwards direction.

In this section we will identify some requirements traceability links that can be used at runtime. To do this we will have a look at some aspects (See Phol [8]) related to requirements traceability, which are summarized in table 1.

Aspect \ Link	Req. - Req.	Req. - Design	Req. - Code	Req. - Test	Req. - Rat.	Req. - Task
During Development Time & Runtime						
Acceptance			D / R	D / R		
Change Mgmt	D / R	D / R	D / R	D / R	D / R	
Quality Mgmt			D / R	D		
Re-Use	D	D	D / R	D	D	
Allocation			D / R			D
Only During Development Time						
Gold Plating		D	D			
Reengineering		D	D	D	D	
Risk Mgmt	D		D			
Project Progr.		D	D	D		D
Process Mgmt						D

Table 1. Traceability Links at runtime, D = usage in dev. R = usage at runtime [7]

The aspects in Table 1. represent different benefits of the availability of traceability links. According to Pohl [8] this table can be used as a basis to identify typical usage of traceability links. As shown in table 1 we only consider the following links:

1. Requirements to Requirements (Req.-Req.)
2. Requirements to Design (Req.-Design)
3. Requirements to Code (Req.-Code)
4. Requirements to Test (Req.-Test)
5. Requirements to Rational (Req.-Rat)

As we can see on table 1 the most important links at runtime are Req.- Code and Req.-Test. If we have to update the code at runtime, the relevant test cases are directly identified. Running these built-in tests at runtime ensures the quality of the software.

Strengths

1. *Supports change management.*
   Any change can be traced and managed correctly.

8

2. *Supports quality management.*
   As any code change is followed by the execution of according built-in test, we can make sure that the change works correctly. Quality remains the same.
3. *Impact analyzis.*
   Any impact of the updated code or requirement can be easily identified using existing traceability links.

Limitations and disadvantages

1. *Requires development effort.*
   During development time we have to generate traceability links and build-in tests which require some additional time and development effort.
2. *Requires build-in test and management effort.*
   To ensure that the changes are correct, build-in tests must be available. These will be executed after each update of the code. The software gets much complex and bigger. Also a lot of management effort is required to maintain the build-in tests and traceability links if they have to be updated, extended or changed over time.

4.3   Active Rules

Using Active Rules to dynamically update a running software is a new framework introduced by Daniel et. al. [10] in their recent work. This framework is basically used in web applications to update them at runtime, in case of a requirement violation. At development time different rules are created using a new introduced language called ECA-WEB [10]. Any rule contains five categories to define scope, events, conditions, the action to be executed and the priority. Figure 2 shows an overview of the framework.

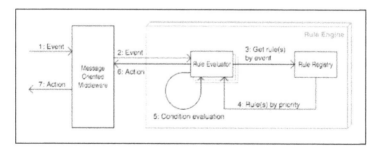

Fig. 2. The rule engine: internal rule execution logic. [10]

As we can see in figure 2 the framework contains a rule engine to manage the rules and a message oriented middleware to communicate with the application. The rule engine contains a rule evaluator to evaluate the rules and a rule registry containing all predefined rules. The engine is embedded in the software [10]. In case of a requirement violation at runtime, e.g. current browser version is not compatible with a feature of the application, an event is raised (1). Using the message oriented middleware the event is processed to the rule evaluator (2). According to the raised event the evaluator picks the right rule from the repository (3). E.g. a rule with scope = browser, web event, conditions to check the session of the user, action to use another similar feature which is supported by that specific browser version and a high priority as the feature is not usable with that browser. The engine checks the rule priority (4) and evaluates the conditions (5). The according action is forwarded to the message driven middleware. At the end the action is executed in the web application (7).

Strengths

1. *Dynamically update the application.*
   The framework makes it possible to dynamically update a running web application at runtime.
2. *Easy to understand.*
   The concepts, rule engine and the rule language are easy to understand and to be implemented.
3. *Rules can be managed dynamically.*
   The framework provides a decoupled environment to administrate the rules. One can add new rules, delete or modify existing rules at runtime [10].

Limitations and disadvantages

1. *Embedded inside the design model.*
   Having an additional software component in the design model makes it much complex and not easy to manage over time.
2. *New language ECA-Web for the rules is introduced.*
   New language in the development environment always requires efforts to understand and learn.
3. *Requires management effort.*
   As part of the application the rule engine has to be managed and maintained over time. Old rules have to be updated or removed over time. Any change in the software should also consider a change in the rules.

4.4   Log-File Analysis

The logs are the language of the application at runtime. Any value of a specific parameter or condition at runtime can be easily written on a log file. Analyzing the log files can help us to identify requirements violations or even identify new requirements. To be able to extract relevant information out of the log files some relevant steps are required. At development time requirement relevant logs should be considered in the programing process. If we know that a specific feature might have a problem at runtime, all relevant parameters should be written in the log file. E.g. if we have a web application and don't know how it will behave on a smart phone, we should write log files where we consider information like platform, browser version, browser name, name of the function called, etc. Having such kind of information could help us to identify requirements violations, performance issues, usability issues etc. All possible improvements can be implemented in the following software release. At runtime the application might generate big log files. To have an overview on the logs available, relevant log entries should be filtered. This requires additional tools to analyze them and filter accordingly. The following graphic shows an overview of how this method can be used.

On the first step we collect the relevant log files out of existing application deployments. On a second step the files are filtered according to requirements relevant log files. On a third step the filtered data is processed on a database and used for requirements analysis.

Disadvantages

Log files might get big (GBs of logs). Analyzing them requires analyzer tools. It requires development effort to specify requirement specific log files.

4.5 Integrated Feedback Tools

Many applications provide the possibility to add new tools and features as additional components. Adding feedback tools as a new feature gives us the possibility to receive feedback directly from the end user. This feedback can be a simple comment, a bug report, a claim, a suggestion to increase usability, something that is not working correctly on his special device etc. Having this kind of feedback can help us to identify new requirements, refine or update the existing requirements. A collection of all feedbacks will then be considered while implementing the next release of the application.

Let' s have a look at a simple example. An end-user tries to open a web-application on his new smart phone. He realizes that the colors are quite different than on his desktop PC. He opens the feedback tool and writes a simple comment with a remark that the colors look quite different and that he can not reed the text correctly.

Also questionnaires and surveys can be integrated and used at runtime.

Disadvantages

1. *Users are fatigue.*
   Users are tired of giving feedback. Even there is a bug or error that can be improved most of users don' t want to give any feedback as they simply feel uncomfortable.
2. *Interpretation of the feedback is not always simple.*
   Having the feedback is one thing, but understanding what the user exactly wants to say is another thing. It is not always simple to interpret it correctly. It might be something totally different from what the end user exactly requires to that what the developers can extract out of it.
3. *Complexity of the application increases.*
   Having feedback tools means having more code in the application. It should be maintained and improved over time, which requires more development effort.

4.6   Interoperability-Log Analysis

The same way as analyzing the logs of the application can also analyze the logs of interoperability modules. If our application interoperates with different external modules, the exchange data format might change over time. Analyzing the according log files can help us identify this kind of log files and change the application accordingly.

Disadvantages

As mentioned in chapter 4.3 one big disadvantage of log files is that they might get too big and require log analyzer tools to gather requirement engineering specific information out of it. Another disadvantage in this special case is that the log files might not always be available and ready to be analyzed.

5   Future Work and Challanges

One of the most important and key issues of run-time requirements engineering is that context and environment is continuously changing. This requires that the requirements are continuously refined and the system behavior is adapted to the changing context. To make this possible, the system must know about its context and environment. Any change should be represented at runtime. Context and environment information must be present in a way that it is understandable for both, the system and the users who interact with the system. It also should be possible to easy manipulate it at runtime. Some of the presented frameworks do have these capabilities, but there is still a lot of work to do. The frameworks are not fully finalized. Monitoring a system at runtime also requires requirements information to be available. As requirements can change over time, it is important that requirements information can be accessed and continuously manipulated at runtime. There must be a standard protocol on how to update the requirements at runtime, so the systems can do this automatically and independent. It would be also much easier for monitoring framework to monitor the system and detect possible requirements valuations. One possible idea would be to have a standard description format for describing requirements, e.g. xml. The specific fields and values that might change during the runtime, due to requirements change, should be accessible and manipulatable by the user and other systems. One can simply change these relevant parameters in the xml description and the system would get an event and change its behavior according to the new requirements. To support this idea, also some design specific aspects at development time must be considered. The system should be capable of reading the manipulated variables at runtime. This might be a challenge as we can not predict any change of the environment, but at least it should cover most relevant requirements. Monitoring frameworks would be able to easily update the xml data according to the discovered changes. Having permanently all changed requirements (in a simple standard format so that all the systems can understand) at runtime, is one of the most important topics which requires some more research. It should be possible to provide a set of mechanisms for representing context in context aware services. All device vendors should have a common understanding on the concepts and should not care about supporting different formats. One open question and important work to do is to find a set of frameworks to be applicable at any kind of software. It should be customizable and easy to understand so that any software developer can bring it in the software engineering process.

6 Conclusion

In this paper I first gave an overview of requirements engineering process at development time. I switched to requirements engineering at runtime focusing on the monitoring technique. I illustrated some existing frameworks in the context of OnlineRE and focused on three main techniques and frameworks. I showed how we can monitor and update the monitoring configuration of an application using PlatoRE. I introduced the technique of traceability links to trace the changes from the code to the requirements and the other way round and explained how adaptive rules can be used in an online requirement engineering context. For each framework. I also showed its strengths, limitations and disadvantages.

References

1. S. Fickas and M.S. Feather: Requirements monitoring in dynamic environments, in RE 95: Proceeding of the Second IEEE International Symposium on Requirements Engineering. Washington, DC, USA: IEEE Computer Society, 1995, pp.140-147
2. Ander J.Ramirez, Betty Cheng and Philip K. McKinley: Adaptive Monitoring of Software Requirements.. Michigan State University, US. IEEE , 2010
3. Daniel M. Berry, U Waterloo Betty H.C. Cheng, Michigan State U Ji Zhang: The Four Levels of Requirements Engineering for and in Dynamic Adaptive Systems. Michigan State U., 2005
4. K. Yue. What Does It Mean to Say that a Specification is Complete? In Proceedings of IWSSD-4 - the Fourth Inter- national Workshop on Software Specification and Design, Monterey, CA, USA, 1987
5. Anthony Finkelstein and Andrea Savigni: A Framework for Requirements Engineering for Context-Aware Services. Department of Computer Science University College London Gower Street London WC1E 6BT United Kingdom, 2010
6. A. Dardenne, A. van Lamsweerde, and S. Fickas. Goal-directed Requirements Acquisition. Science of Computer Programming, 20:3 - 50, 1993.
7. Alexander Delater, Barbara Peach. Using Requirements Traceability Links at Runtime. University of Heidelberg, Institute of Computer Science. Heidelberg. Germany, 2010
8. Pohl, K.: Requirements Engineering, dpunkt.verlag. 2008
9. Gotel, O., Finkelstein, A.: An Analysis of the Requirements Traceability Problem. In: Proceedings of the International Conference on Requirements Engineering, Colorado Springs, CO, USA, pp. 94,Äì 101 (1994)
10. Florian Daniel, Maristella Matera, Alessandro Morandi, Matteo Mortari, and Giuseppe Pozzi: Active Rules for Runtime Adaptivity Management. Dipartimento di Elettronica e Informazione, Politecnico di Milano. Italy, 2010
11. Andres J. Ramirez,David B. Knoester, Betty H.C. Cheng, Philip K. McKinley: Plato: a genetic algorithm approach to run-time reconfiguration in autonomic computing systems, 2010
URL:www.cse.msu.edu/ dk/papers/ramirez2010plato.pdf (Access 02.03.2011)

14

YOUR KNOWLEDGE HAS VALUE